MW00993335

Clever Island

TECHNOLOGY AND NATURE

David Drew

Illustrated by Peter Gouldthorpe

RIGBY

~ Contents ~

I found myself on Clever Island ~ 3

On Clever Island I found:

some palm leaves ~ 4
some coconuts ~ 5
some shells ~ 6
a clam shell ~ 7
some seed pods ~ 8
some seaweed ~ 9
some sticks ~ 10
some vines ~ 11
some fish bones ~ 12
a bird skeleton ~ 13
some reeds ~ 14
some bamboo ~ 15

I was found on Clever Island ~ 16

*I found myself on
Clever Island.*

On Clever Island I found some
PALM LEAVES.
How can I use them to make:
a sun hat, *or*
a shelter, *or*
cooking foil?

What else will I need?

2

9

1

3

4

5

6

8

10

On Clever Island I found some
CONUTS.
How can I use them to make:
a vase, *or*
a cup, *or*
a raft?

A key to the island is on page 17

11
12
13
14
15
16
17
18
19
20
21
22
23

On Clever Island I found some **SHELLS**.

How can I use them to make:

a needle, *or*

a fish hook, *or*

a necklace?

What else will I need?

On Clever Island I found a
CLAM SHELL.
How can I use it to make:
a knife, *or*
a fish scaler, *or*
a cooking pot?

A key to the island is on page 17

On Clever Island I found some
SEED PODS.

How can I use them to make:
a musical instrument, *or*
a calendar, *or*
a ruler?

What else will I need?

On Clever Island I found some
SEAWEED.
How can I use it to make:
a cushion, *or*
a belt, *or*
a barometer?

A key to the island is on page 17

11
12
13
14
15
16
17
18
19
20
21
22
23

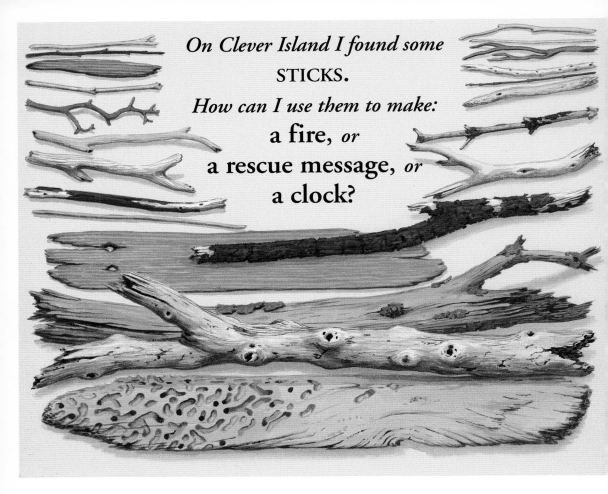

On Clever Island I found some STICKS.

How can I use them to make:
a fire, *or*
a rescue message, *or*
a clock?

What else will I need?

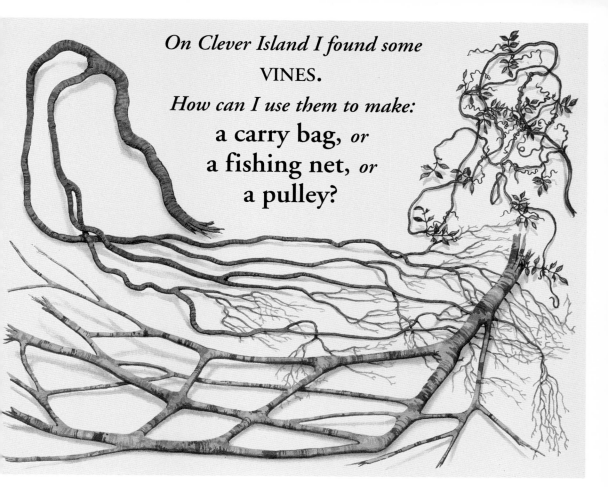

On Clever Island I found some
VINES.
How can I use them to make:
a carry bag, *or*
a fishing net, *or*
a pulley?

A key to the island is on page 17

11

12   13   14

15   16

17   18   19   20   21   22   23

On Clever Island I found some
FISH BONES.
How can I use them to make:
a comb, *or*
a pin, *or*
a pair of tweezers?

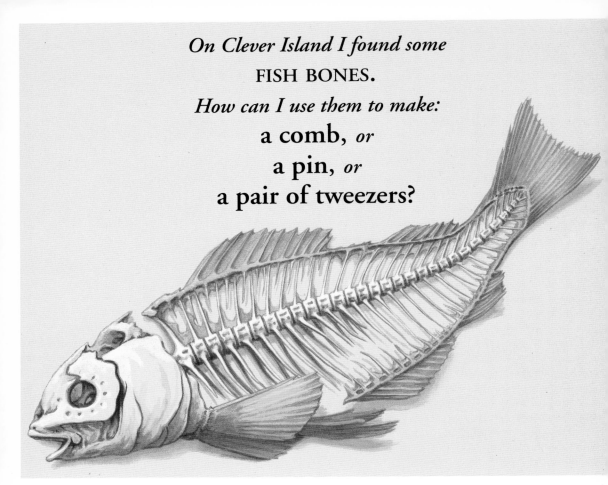

What else will I need?

On Clever Island I found a
BIRD SKELETON.
How can I use it to make:
a drinking straw, *or*
a pencil, *or*
a quill pen?

A key to the island is on page 17

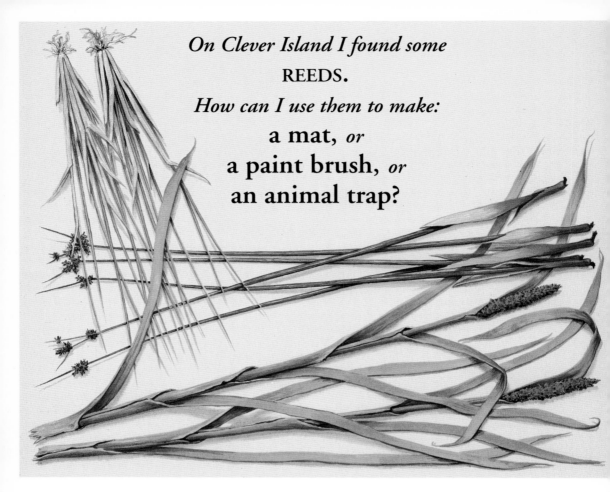

On Clever Island I found some
REEDS.
How can I use them to make:
a mat, *or*
a paint brush, *or*
an animal trap?

What else will I need?

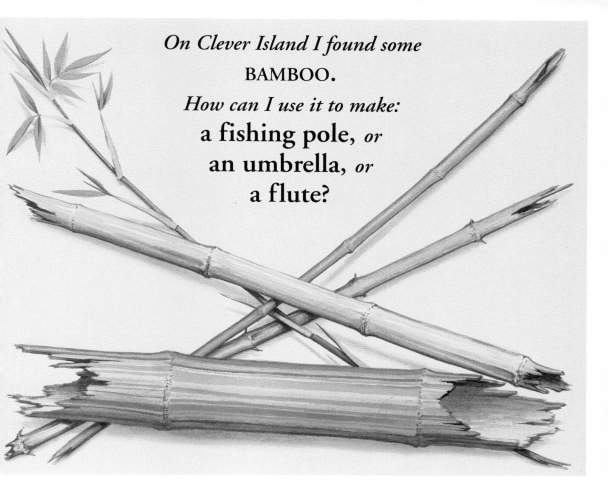

On Clever Island I found some
BAMBOO.

How can I use it to make:
a fishing pole, *or*
an umbrella, *or*
a flute?

A key to the island is on page 17

11
12
13
14
15
16
17
18
19
20
21
22
23

I was found on
Clever Island.